THE LIBRARY OF
WOLVES AND WILD DOGS ™

THE
DINGO

Janice Koler-Matznick

The Rosen Publishing Group's
PowerKids Press ™
New York

To Dr. Laurence Corbett, for his work studying dingoes

Published in 2002 by The Rosen Publishing Group, Inc.
29 East 21st Street, New York, NY 10010

First Edition

Book Design: Michael de Guzman
Project Editor: Emily Raabe

Photo Credits: pp. 4, 12 © Fritz Prenzel/Animals Animals; p 7 © John Cancalosi/Peter Arnold, Inc.; p. 9 (top) © Fritz Prenzel/Peter Arnold, Inc.; p. 9 (bottom) © Roland Seitre/Peter Arnold, Inc.; p. 10 © Hans and Judy Beste/Animals Animals; p. 11 © Tom Brakefield/CORBIS; p. 15 © Gerrard Lacz/ Animals Animals; p. 16 (top) © Paul A. Souders/CORBIS; p. 16 (bottom) © Joe McDonald/CORBIS; p. 19 © Rogge, Otto Stock Photos; p. 20 (background) © Diego Lezamo Orezzoli/CORBIS; p. 20 (inset) © Penny Tweedie/CORBIS; p. 22 © Hamman/Heldring/Animals Animals.

Koler-Matznick, Janice.
   The dingo / by Janice Koler-Matznick. —1st ed.
      p. cm. — (The library of wolves and wild dogs)
   ISBN 0-8239-5768-3 (lib. bdg.)
1. Dingo—Juvenile literature. [1. Dingo.] I. Title II. Series.
   QL737.C22 K76 2002
   599.77'2—dc21
                                  00-011860

Manufactured in the United States of America

Contents

A Wild Dog

They might look like pet dogs, but the dingoes of Australia are true wild dogs. Dingoes are relatives of the **domestic** dog and the wolf. One way to tell wolves, dingoes, and domestic dogs apart is by the size of their teeth. Domestic dogs have small teeth compared to those of dingoes and wolves. Dingoes and wolves need big teeth because they have to catch other animals for food. A domestic dog usually does not hunt its own food. Another difference between domestic dogs and dingoes is that, unlike domestic dogs, dingoes almost never bark. Instead of barking, dingoes may yip, howl, or whine to communicate with one another. Dingoes are red, tan, black, or white. They are never gray like some wolves. Pure dingoes are also never white with spots like some domestic dogs.

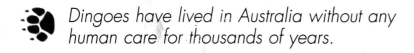

Dingoes have lived in Australia without any human care for thousands of years.

The Mystery of the Dingo

No one knows where dingoes came from. Dingoes look something like the small wolves of India, so the Indian wolf might be the dingo **ancestor**. We also do not know when dingoes were brought to Australia. When people first arrived in Australia, about 40,000 years ago, there were no dingoes there. Australia is surrounded by ocean. At some point, people must have brought dingoes to Australia in boats. The oldest Australian dingo bones found so far are about 4,000 years old. It is hard for scientists to know if these are the oldest dingo bones in Australia. This is because wild animal bones are hard to find. Most of them do not last long. They get chewed by animals and worn down by weather. All scientists know for sure is that dingoes were in Australia at least 4,000 years ago. They might have been there much longer.

Although dingoes and the native people of Australia have shared the country for at least 4,000 years, the dingo has always been, and is still considered, a wild dog.

Different Kinds of Dingoes

There is only one **species** of dingo in Australia, but dingoes from different areas in Australia have bodies that are **adapted** to where they live. Dingoes living in the hot tropics and deserts, for example, have short fur and large ears. This helps them lose body heat and stay cool. Dingoes living in the mountains, where it's cooler, have smaller ears. Their fur gets thick in winter when it is very cold. Small ears and thick hair help the mountain dingoes keep in their body heat. The largest dingoes are found in some forest and grassland areas. These dingoes need to be big to catch large animals such as **kangaroos**.

This Alpine dingo has small, furry ears and thick fur to help it stay warm high in the mountains.

This dingo lives in the desert. It has larger ears and shorter fur than the alpine dingo shown below.

A Closer Look

Like wolves and other wild dogs, dingoes have ears that stand up straight. Their tails are long and slightly curved. Dingoes are about the size of a thin Labrador retriever dog. They are from 20 to 24 inches (51 to 61 cm) tall at the top of their shoulders. Females are smaller than males. Female dingoes weigh from 26 to 40 pounds (12 to 18 kg). Males weigh from 35 to 48 pounds (16 to 22 kg). Most dingoes are reddish brown or tan, but some are black with tan on their legs and face, and a few are white.

Some dingoes are white, like the one shown here.

Nearly all dingoes have white markings on their toes and tail tip. Some dingoes also have white on their chests.

Dingo Groups

How dingoes live depends on the numbers and kinds of **prey** in the area. Prey are the animals that dingoes eat. In places with large animals to hunt, dingoes may live in **packs**. In places with small prey, dingoes live in pairs of one male and one female. Most of the time people see only one or two dingoes in one place, although other dingoes might be hidden nearby. In the desert, different packs sometimes have to share a **water hole**. The two packs will stay far away from each other and take turns getting drinks. At night dingoes in packs often howl a lot. This lets other dingoes know the pack's location.

This pack of dingoes will hunt together to bring down large prey animals such as kangaroos.

Raising Puppies

Dingo mothers have **litters** of about five puppies. Dingo puppies are almost black when they are born. Their adult color grows in over several weeks. Dingoes usually raise their puppies in a **den**. Dens may be holes in the ground. Sometimes a den is inside a hollow log or under a bush. The mother feeds young puppies with her milk. When the puppies are about four weeks old, the parents start to bring them meat. At first the parents eat the meat and carry it in their stomachs to the puppies. When the puppies lick the parents' mouths, the parents push the meat out of their stomachs to feed the pups. Desert dingoes often bring water to the puppies In the same way. When the puppies are about 12 weeks old, the parents start teaching them to hunt. The puppies stay with their parents for several months.

Mother dingoes nurse their pups for about 8 weeks. After 4 weeks, the pups begin to eat some meat along with their mother's milk.

Dingoes Making a Living

Dingoes are **predators**. This means that they eat other animals. What dingoes eat depends on which prey animals live in their area. A pack working together can hunt bigger prey than one dingo could catch by itself. Packs can catch kangaroos, the largest **native** animals in Australia. One big kangaroo has enough meat to feed many dingoes. Most dingoes, however, do not hunt in packs. The animals dingoes eat most often are **wallabies**, small **mammals**, lizards, and birds. Dingoes also hunt the rabbits and pigs that people have turned loose in Australia. This is good, because there are too many **feral** rabbits and pigs in Australia.

Dingoes hunt every day, but they do not always catch something to eat. Many times the prey gets away and dingoes go hungry.

 Feral rabbits (bottom) eat the food that other animals, *such as wallabies (top),* need to survive.

The Dingo Fence

Domestic sheep are easy for a dingo to catch because the sheep can't run very fast. In most sheep areas, farming has removed many of the dingo's native prey. Some dingoes in these areas hunt sheep. To keep dingoes away from the sheep, the people of Australia built the Dingo Fence. The Dingo Fence was started in 1920. It is about 3,320 miles (5,343 km) long and about 6 feet (2 m) high. This fence is the longest fence in the world. People work every day to keep the fence strong. The bottom of the Dingo Fence goes down about 1 foot (.3 m) into the ground to keep dingoes from digging under it. Most of the sheep are raised in the eastern and southern parts of Australia. Because of the Dingo Fence, most of the dingoes in Australia live on the western and northern sides of the fence, where there are less sheep.

The Dingo Fence separates the eastern and southern parts of Australia from the rest of the country.

Dingoes and People

European settlers came to Australia with domestic dogs about 200 years ago. Before that time, the **Aboriginal** people sometimes caught wild dingo puppies and raised them in their camps. The Aboriginal people kept dingoes mostly because they liked their company. Dingoes are hard to train. Most **tamed** dingoes were useful only for helping hunters find small prey. The dingoes actually chased large, fast animals, such as kangaroos, away from the hunters. The dingoes did help to keep the camps clean of garbage, however. This was very useful, because the people did not have someone to collect their garbage. Most dingoes raised in camps went back to the wild when they grew up. Then the people would catch more puppies to raise.

Dingoes and Aboriginal people have lived around each other for thousands of years.

Saving the Dingoes

The biggest threat to dingo survival is the domestic dog. Wild dingoes and domestic dogs are able to breed together. Many people in Australia let their dogs run loose. These dogs sometimes breed with dingoes. Today the few wild dingoes in southern and eastern Australia are mostly mixes of domestic dog and dingo. Pure dingoes are becoming rare. Dingoes probably will become **extinct** unless people save them. Some people in Australia are trying to save the dingo by breeding dingoes to be pets. Although some dingoes can be pets in modern cities, most of them are too wild. The best way to save dingoes is to protect them in the wild. People are working to make places away from domestic dogs and sheep where wild dingoes can live free. The fate of the dingo, one of the oldest kinds of dogs in the world, depends on how much people care about them.

Glossary

Aboriginal (a-beh-RIJ-nal) The first people to live in Australia.

adapted (uh-DAP-tid) Changed to fit in with new conditions.

ancestor (AN-ses-tur) A relative who lived long ago.

den (DEN) A wild animal's home.

domestic (doh-MES-tik) A kind of animal made by people choosing which animals to breed together.

extinct (ik-STINKT) To no longer exist. If an animal is extinct, it means the last one has died.

feral (FER-al) A domestic animal that has gone back to live in the wild.

kangaroos (kan-guh-ROOZ) Animals that eat plants and hop around on their hind legs.

litters (LIH-turz) Groups of baby animals born to the same mother at the same time.

mammals (MA-mulz) Warm-blooded animals that have backbones, are often covered with hair, breathe air, and feed milk to their young.

native (NAY-tiv) Born in a certain place or country.

packs (PAKS) Groups of the same kind of animal hunting or living together.

predators (PREH-duh-terz) An animal that kills other animals for food.

prey (PRAY) An animal that is hunted by other animals for food.

species (SPEE-sheez) A single kind of plant or animal For example, all people are one species.

tamed (TAYMD) To have made a wild animal gentle.

wallabies (WAH-luh-beez) Small kangaroos. Some are as small as rabbits.

water hole (WAH-ter HOHL) A pond or another place where there is water for animals to drink.

Index

Web Sites

For more information about dingoes, check out these Web sites:
www.canids.org/SPPACCTS/dingo.htm
www.dingosanctuary.org/
www.wwwins.net.au/dingofarm/